Jade's Secret Ingredients

A RECIPE FOR MANAGING FEELINGS

written by
Ashley Finley

JJ CARSON PRESS

illustrated by
Agia Putri

Jade's Secret Ingredients: A Recipe for Managing Feelings

Published by JJ Carson Press, LLC

8553 North Beach Street, Suite 110

Keller, Texas, 76244

www.jjcarsonpress.com

ISBN HARDBACK: 978-1-7369724-1-0

ISBN PAPERBACK: 978-1-7369724-0-3

To my husband, Kris.

Thank you for always encouraging me to

chase my wildest dreams.

Hi! My name is Jade, and I love baking,
but I don't just bake with anyone.
My granny is my favorite baking buddy.

Together,

we bake all kinds of delicious foods.

Granny's Goodies Bakery

My granny is the best baker around.

You can ask anyone.

We all love her cookies, breads, and cakes.

Of course, I love all of Granny's treats,

but what I love the most

is the time we spend together.

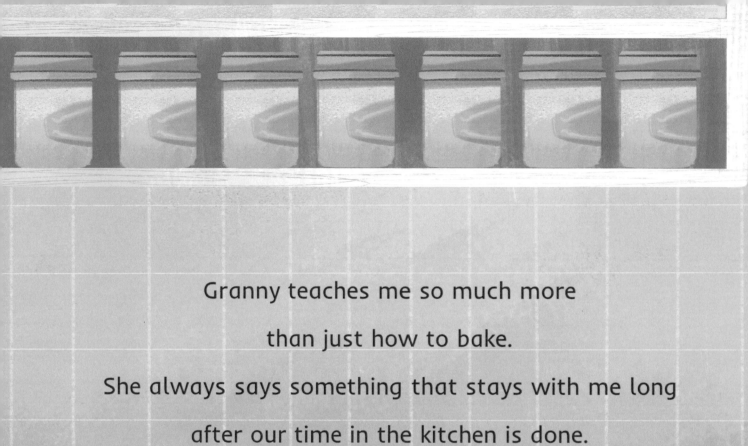

Granny teaches me so much more
than just how to bake.
She always says something that stays with me long
after our time in the kitchen is done.
These are our secret ingredients.

Secret Ingredient #1: Stay In The Moment

When Granny and I bake together,

sometimes I start to think of all the steps that I need

to complete and get confused along the way.

"Just do one step at a time," she'll tell me.

"This way, you don't get ahead of yourself and miss

the chance to enjoy each moment."

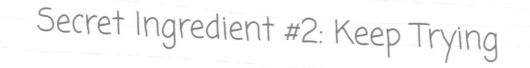

Secret Ingredient #2: Keep Trying

At times, when we bake, I make mistakes.

Granny takes her time and helps me look at

them in a positive way.

"How can you turn those mistakes into

something delicious?" she'll ask.

Secret Ingredient #3: Have Fun

Mixing can be fun,

and sometimes I get carried away.

It's easy to get flour all over the place.

Granny will chuckle and whisper in my ear,

"Sometimes making a mess is the

best part, my dear."

Secret Ingredient #4: Take Breaks

When things get hard and I feel like giving up,

Granny will flash her bright smile and say,

"You're doing so well, honey.

But, it looks like it's time to give yourself a break.

Make sure you come back and finish.

You'll be glad you did."

On some days,

I get curious and ask lots of questions.

Granny always responds with love and says,

"That's one of my favorite things about you.

You are always brave enough to ask."

Secret Ingredient #6: Be Patient

When I look into the oven and want to

take out our baked goodies too soon,

Granny will say,

"Patience is important, my love.

Our treats aren't done just yet.

Come, let's play a game while we wait."

Although I love baking with Granny,

it makes me frustrated when I can't get something right.

"Close your eyes, take a deep breath," Granny calmly says,

"Count backward with me.

5... 4... 3... 2... 1...

Now open your eyes and try your best.

Practice makes progress."

Secret Ingredient #8: Reflect

When we finish baking our treats,

Granny will often say,

"Let's stand back and look at all we have done.

Every ingredient played a part in making

this wonderful new creation.

Each one is just as important as the others."

Secret Ingredient #9: Be Thankful

Sometimes things come out the way that we planned,
and other times they turn out differently.
No matter the result, Granny always gives me a hug
and happily says, "I'm so grateful that I was able to
bake with you today."

All of these secret ingredients are special,

just like each ingredient in a recipe.

The best thing about these special ingredients is

that I can take them with me everywhere I go –

to school, to the mall, to the park.

No matter where I am, I have the power to use these secret ingredients myself and to share them with others.

Jade's Secret Ingredients

Secret Ingredient #1: Stay In The Moment

Secret Ingredient #2: Keep Trying

Secret Ingredient #3: Have Fun

Secret Ingredient #4: Take Breaks

Secret Ingredient #5: Ask Questions

Secret Ingredient #6: Be Patient

Secret Ingredient #7: Relax

Secret Ingredient #8: Reflect

Secret Ingredient #9: Be Thankful

CPSIA information can be obtained
at www.ICGtesting.com
Printed in the USA
LVRC101001010921
696671LV00005B/11